Town Cats

Town Cats

JOHN WEBB

MICHAEL JOSEPH
LONDON

First published in Great Britain by
Michael Joseph Ltd, 44 Bedford Square, London WC1
1980

ISBN 0 7181 1968 1

Filmset and printed by
BAS Printers Limited, Over Wallop, Hampshire
and bound by
Hunter & Foulis Ltd., Edinburgh

My parents once had a cat who regularly brought home conference pears. Another I met presented, over a period of weeks, a succession of live goldfish. Yet another, golf balls.

I deduced from all this that cats *are* capable of unselfish acts, a concept astonishing to me and therefore deserving of further attention.

Living with a cat, I soon learned that he had facial expressions as obvious as any actor's. Hunger, greed, contentment, fatigue, smugness, indifference, anger, contempt, curiosity, indigestion, resentment and levity, all paraded across his features with theatrical conspicuousness.

Most of his actions, I admit, erred on the side of self-interest. But once, when I was ill with a brain tumour or lung cancer—I forget which—he slept on the bed under my chin. He'd never done this before, and I was later told it was to keep me warm and hasten the return of health. My scepticism suggested rather a concern on his part about the apparent frailty of his source of dinners. The surprising thing was though, he *did* it.

After this I realised cats were more complex than I had dreamed possible. Maybe, with familiarity, one discerns an equal sophistication in budgerigars and hamsters, but I doubt it. Anyway, I decided to observe cats in future with positive tolerance and circumspection. I almost added: respect.

But it never went quite that far.

This is Hodge, named after Dr. Johnson's pampered mog. Contrary to some opinion, cats do answer to their names, although their ability to discriminate between consonants is questionable. Hodge reacts equally enthusiastically, for instance, to Stodge, Dodge, Splodge, Wodge, etc.

Two years ago the rightful owner of this cat discovered she was sharing its favours with three other households in the area. In all, four families were deluding themselves that it belonged to them. The cat apportioned its time with care and commendable fairness, slipping in and out daily for the odd snack or nap. When the extent of its infidelity was made public, a party was organised in the square in its honour, merely exemplifying, I'm afraid, our secret admiration for the successful fraud.

Cats have difficulty sustaining the demeanour their social status demands. This one, I happen to know, had brunched five minutes earlier on quails' breasts in aspic and lightly poached turbot.

11

If you plead long enough with a door it will eventually open. However, it takes a long time if you've only just been let out, and even longer if you've got a ridiculous white tip on the end of your tail. You can appeal to passers-by, but that rarely has any effect except if it's an old lady with cherries on her hat and a basket on wheels. Why is it one wants to be out when one is in, and vice versa? Why can't people just leave doors sensibly ajar? There's nothing worth pinching in the house anyway.

A lot of cats object to strangers clumping round the house. This one whose name, improbably, is Faith, demonstrates displeasure ostrich-fashion. The crashing and whistling of decorators on this day caused the lump to flinch occasionally, although Faith was clearly secure in the conviction that her very existence remained undetected.

15

If you look hard and long enough you'll always find somewhere another cat looking hard and long at the hard and long-looking cat which you are looking hard and long at.

A cat's equivalent of wearing dark glasses is to peer furtively at things from behind other things. Leaves are particulary suitable because they make you feel primitive and virile and earthy. Like having a cigarette in the corner of your mouth on top of (or, rather, below) the sunglasses. Cats invented the cool, recondite exterior, and none needs Freud to help him understand himself.

When you watch a cat displaying its infinite capacity for staring out of a window, notice its head movements. There will be a succession of intent small jerks as his attention is distracted from one amazing sight to another. After five minutes of it, you are convinced there has been a murder outside the front door, that a platoon of Russian infantry has passed, a zebra been savaged by hyenas and a parachutist landed. Look out of the window yourself and you'll see a totally silent, deserted street.

21

Cats are unrelenting grudge-harbourers. When aggrieved or disgusted they frequently present an exterior like a sack of nuts. This fellow's owners had had the insensitivity to come home late the previous night, which caused breakfast to be equally late. His unattractive back was all they saw of the cat the following day. He forgave them though, magnanimously, round about dinner-time.

This chilling expression, at once censorious and contemptuous, gives credence to the belief that cats only pretend to be a lesser species and that really they're ruthlessly using us to their own ends. The theory could explain why, when you've had a hard, frustrating day trying to earn a living and, coming home, have just been caught in the rain, a cat will often stretch and give a quiet snigger.

Cats hate going into cars. They usually associate them with visits to vets which mean injections, painful probes up unmentionable places, disinfectant smells and humans in white coats who handle you like lumpy parcels, unimpressed by your oaths and menaces, poking torches in your mouth and making you swallow small white things. And your owner, whom you love and protect, just stands there and lets them!

This anxious fellow knows he is clearly on his way to a vivisectionist, Dachau, the knacker's yard or a pop concert.

A window is a wonderful thing. It lets you take part as an observer in a million adventures and liaisons without moving far from a radiator or a kitchen. And when you feel like a nap, which is most of the time, there are no breezes or spots of cold rain. Usually, windows keep out other cats as well; a sensible arrangement.

Cats can't resist entertaining visitors. Their natural high spirits always get the better of them, particularly after a heavy meal. This witty and absorbing fellow keeps friends and neighbours amused by his drolleries at any and every hour of the day.

If you look closely you can not only see the cat but also the key to the picture's message. It can be discerned in the form of a white package between the two men. Lunch.

An early sign of spring, a first, warm glaze of sunshine, and even the more cynical among us feel a certain kindly regard for our fellow creatures and, more importantly, ourselves.

One of the feline virtues is an unerring aesthetic judgement, when appropriate, about looking one's best. Hodge, for instance, will often choose a sunbeam to sit in, preferably with a tapestry as backdrop, wearing a foppish and revolting smirk. He leaves small bottom-marks, though, like finger-prints, on the polish of our 18th century forte-piano.

A cat which is situated higher than its neighbours has a distinct (to him) advantage. The dominant cat in a room will always contrive to get on top of something, perhaps so that other cats there have to look up. A more likely reason, though, is a natural and appropriate desire to be nearer God.

The first time I met this cat, the Volkswagen was doing about forty in front of us. The cat was slithering about on top, claws out trying to get a grip on the paintwork. At some lights I informed the driver who gave a look of infinite tiredness, sighed and said, "Not again", put the cat inside, did a three-point turn and raced back the way he'd come.

This Teutonic cat's territorial claims loom large over him. Don't let his slow, country bumpkin demeanour deceive you. Because he's got a silly smudge on his nose doesn't mean his head's not full of Wagnerian theories of expansion and the conquest of the weak by the mighty. When it comes to defence, he has ways of making you balk.

OVERLEAF
Autumn's the best time to live in a London square. When you're turfed out in crude daylight, at least there are leaves which saunter past that could be prey, and stupid things which drop out of trees. It's quieter, too. You can hear that old fool practising the flute quite clearly. Cars arrive and depart, with all their concomitant noise and activity, less frequently. You're allowed back in earlier, but let out later, for some reason, more reluctantly. Altogether it's a season of repose and dignity. Nights are full of decision and forward-planning.

Winter, needless to say, is a different story.

As I passed this window, a cultivated male voice from inside called, "Who's his daddy's baby panther then?" The cat simpered smugly and left the windowsill, spoiling the shot somewhat.

Siamese cats are clever at climbing people. That's why their owners invariably have very thick skin. It helps defend them as well from the continual barrage of complaint the cats feel it necessary to utter in their loud baritone voices.

I'm not sure which way the dog is facing. At first, I thought it was a shredded wheat shop display, until one end took a detailed interest in some wet on the wall.

43

Cats like to play the role of sentinel. It appeals to the archaic in their natures. They're very old-fashioned, really. They accept cars, provided they don't have to go in them, with resignation and faint disapproval, are polite to elderly ladies in flowery frocks, tolerant of well-behaved children, milkmen and pigeons, but hate intensely ice cream vans with chimes, loud motor-bikes and young men kicking Kentucky Fried Chicken cartons and shouting, particularly after most decent folk are in bed.

Parked cars are to cats what hedgerows are to birds, a thoroughfare, an ambuscade, a sanctuary. There's hardly an urban pavement now without its automotive hedge. A tribute to cats' fleetness of foot is that more are not run over as people start off for Tesco's or picnics on the A4. Motorists who have dirt on their foreheads and knees are the prudent, circumspect ones.

Point 1: Predominantly-black cats always have odd, white, stiff hairs, like misplaced whiskers, here and there.

Point 2: Cats like to station themselves at the junction of scenarios where they can watch, for instance, what's happening at street level and also the basement door, just in case someone loses his sanity and runs amok dispensing duck pâté, kipper fillets and sucking pigs with apples in their mouths.

Cats like birds. They like to get a close look at them. It's purely the curiosity of the naturalist and playmate. People accuse cats of killing birds and sometimes of eating them, but this is all due to the bird's frailty and a cat's natural desire to remove evidence of any accident likely to attract opprobrium or grief in humans.

Another mystery is: why do blue-tits keep away when a friendly Siamese is examining their roof? Perhaps someone will do a book on Town Birds and elucidate.

In Holland Park, there's another city among the roofs. At night we're put in mind of burglars by occasional elephantine thumps. It seems, when they're not watched, cats forego all their customary lightness and grace. All manners, too. The gravelled roof outside our kitchen window serves now merely as a communal lavatory. And there's an urn of ruined begonias above us that has clearly become someone's bed. Not long ago, an old tom went through a sky-light nearby, landed in an upholstered chair, deemed the whole thing remarkably fortuitous, curled up and went to sleep.

Cats have to get into things. No cat can pass a paper bag or empty carton without testing its potentiality as a nest. A neighbour's cat always sleeps in a grapefruit box. His owner once lined it with newspaper, imagining he was doing the cat a favour. The cat glowered reproachfully from the top of a wardrobe for three days until the paper was removed.

Cats are sensitive creatures, easily offended by breaches of etiquette or lapses in taste. Anyone whose attributes, particularly in matters of physical shape or sartorial sense, are in doubt attracts censorious appraisal mingled with disbelief.

OVERLEAF
This chap is remarkable only for his sexual proclivities. I have seen him several times make passionate love to a small bay tree near us. While he embraces it and rubs his face in its leaves he dribbles and purrs. It's quite disgusting.

55

All markets have cats. They slide quite naturally into the life-style of costermongers, adopting with ease the appropriate attitudes and mannerisms, the eschewing of fastidiousness, the preoccupation with gain, the derisive turn of phrase and the dog-end behind the ear. Evading customers' feet is another important talent, particularly when the feet are large and are moving swiftly in the direction of their rear-ends.

Cats are no greedier than other animals. They just seem that way. At a dinner party, Hodge, for example, will intuitively recognise the soft-touches. He wheedles round them, looking pitifully undernourished and generally deprived, one of life's victims, unwanted, succumbing bravely to the final throes of malnutrition. A magnificently touching performance worthy of the Royal Shakespeare Company.

He won't even bother with a conspirational wink when he catches my cynical eye. He accepts as his due the "Aaaahs" and "The-e-eres" of the diners together with large portions of the contents of their plates.

It's curious though that, despite his apparent invalidism, he manages to separate and discard the tiniest fragments of brussels sprout.

Attempts to keep cats out of somewhere guarantee their attempts to get in. The best way to deter cats is to stick welcome notices everywhere, fill the place with little open doors and bridges and ladders.

A house nearby used to be sealed hermetically against the entry of a virulently smelly tom who claimed ownership of the place. For months, mysteriously, he used to get in. Eventually they bricked up the chimney, and that was that.

There are two barges on an Amsterdam canal where hundreds of strays live. They are very sleek and fat, and well-mannered and are looked after by a band of nice, dedicated human servants. There are also a couple of large, patient dogs who plod about philosophically with cats riding on their backs.

When a cat does something clumsy it conceals its embarrassment with a brief burst of washing. This is supposed to indicate to the world at large its indifference and the fact that, if you're so bored and unintelligent as to have nothing better to do than watch clumsy cats, the clumsiness was quite deliberate anyway.

I know this cat. It's one of the type that runs up to you in the street for a spot of affection, and when you stroke it, hisses and retreats with lashing tail as if you'd made an improper suggestion or picked its pocket. I don't know if it's female. Probably.

It's no accident that cats have cup-shaped faces. Millions of years of natural selection have produced the perfect tool for hoovering up sugary tea-grouts. They're also the right shape for levering open doors although not for closing them again. Darwinists are working on it.

Black cats are shamelessly proud of their stomachs, and are generous about displaying them to passers-by, particularly when the weather is warm and it involves rolling on to something unseemly.

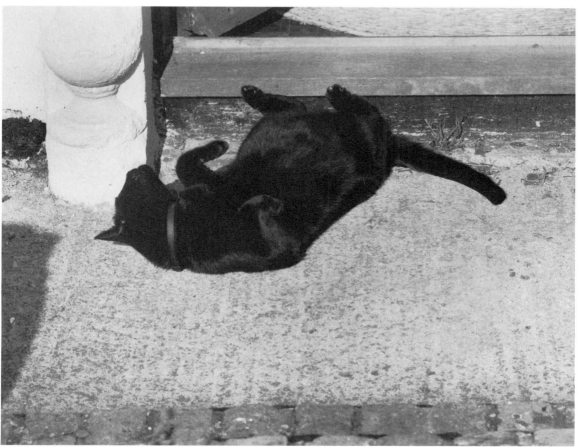

This is Tiddles. I know it's Tiddles because an anxious female voice intones his name every night endlessly, and because I once saw him imprisoned behind a window of her house. She calls in vain, I assume, and hasn't yet learned the value as a blandishment of the tin struck with an opener or the clash of saucer on kitchen floor.

Cats from warm climates are smaller and thinner than their northern European relations. I don't know if they've evolved genetically to appear less tempting for culinary consideration or simply get less to eat themselves. This fellow was one of a number of cats living in the Valetta botanical gardens which, interestingly, boasts more bowls of food than it does rare plants.

The fact that so many idle men wander about photographing cats is the reason for the lack of surprise, not to say boredom, on this fellow's face. He's seen it all before, people with little black, clicking things that they push against their faces and duck and dart about with. Even more ridiculous are the big sheets of paper some people hold in front of them when they're sitting down indoors, and the metal sticks they play with food with, sleeping on enormous padded ledges, staring at a noisy, flickering box . . . it's endless.

What I said, wandering down a street in Nicosia ("Hello, you're a handsome fellow"), didn't deserve, I thought, to be greeted with quite such indifference. After all, I was only trying to ingratiate myself. But perhaps the cat understood only Greek. Or Turkish.

If only, at parties, you could disengage yourself from a bore with equal decisiveness and unconcern for feelings, how honest and strong you would feel. Vulnerable, too, I suppose, to being beaten up later on the street corner.

Cats are not very good at discerning openings. If you make a tunnel in the carpet and toss a paper ball down it (leafing through this book, you obviously spend an inordinate amount of time at such trivia), your moggy will at first try to retrieve it through the *roof* of the tunnel. It quickly becomes frustrated with biting and scrabbling and trying to kill the tunnel with its back legs. So, after a quick wash to show its repudiation of the concept of failure, the painful process of thought takes place. The ball went in *there.* But now it is roughly *there.*

Don't make light of this situation when it occurs. It's one of the few where you're justified in a slight sense of superiority.

A cat's expression is often marred by its markings. A splosh of white across an otherwise black cat's face, however angry or plaintive it is pretending to be, always makes it look frivolous and slightly absurd. This cat's outrage at my trespassing comes across merely as mild surprise and curiosity, tempered by the confession that it is simple-minded and therefore not to be taken seriously.

Cats like acknowledgement of their existence in the form, when they can attract it, of permanent attention. This subject has perfected the courtesan's art of seduction, the languorous recumbency, the tantalising glance, the whispered entreaty. Three-quarters of an hour separated these two shots, during which time McCann Erickson lost forty-five minutes of copywriting productivity.

When you look at a thing sideways it means you're not taking it seriously; you're indulging in a little donnish joke. The dry aphorism, the trenchant facetiousness, the gay drollery, the Wildean epigram, the sardonic badinage are all a fulsome part of a cat's make up.

Just as Roget's Thesaurus is of mine.

Keeping a garden in order is a lot of work. A cat is useful here, being often prepared a couple of times a day to lend a zealous paw with such chores as digging out irritating crocus and hyacinth bulbs or tidily levelling beds of otherwise unruly aubrietia. With judicious use of territory a cat at its toilet can eradicate troublesome weeds like clematis and ceanothus in a matter of days.

When you summon a cat he will invariably flinch and ignore you. Call a couple of times more, and eventually, in his own time, he will respond, strolling with studied indifference towards you. Halfway, he will pause, yawn and stretch his back legs, just in case you were under the illusion that he really wanted to come across. When, at length, he arrives at your feet, the sensible thing is to kick him up the backside. It won't teach him to behave more reasonably, but its a marvellous way of releasing tension.

Stairs are good for tripping a person up on. Especially if he's carrying something heavy. The person often hurts himself or panics but always uses a lot of bad language. Cats, however, are seldom scathed by these encounters. They shout a warning before the unwary foot touches them, dart niftily aside and are then aghast at man's ungainliness and accident-proneness. Having attracted attention, they use the situation to beg a snack or cuddle, pleas which are seldom heeded for some reason in these circumstances.

This was the friendliest cat I've met. The problem was to keep it far enough away for a shot. I tried to get the first ever exposure of a cat climbing up the photographer's trouser-leg, but he moved too fast. In a break in his overtures, however, he displayed the cat's warmth of feeling for vehicles that are stationary and silent.

Patrolling his territory is one of a cat's daily chores. Favourite vantage points vary, but have to be places where the sun falls. There he can doze and picket his property at the same time. In the winter this reconnaissance is less rigorously observed. We assume that the presence of warmth and comfort are as important an ingredient in this ritual as in all others.

Have you ever seen a cat manifest affection when it's just been fed? Demonstrations of love tend to be inseparable from pangs of hunger. A human with such transparently questionable ethics would be stood up against a wall by his neighbours in the interests of social propriety.

In France cats seem more diffident than in Britain, queueing in panic to escape the presumption and boredom of my attentions. So presumptuous and boring, it would appear, is the average Englishman that a crack no bigger than a letterbox will do. Maybe they're like it with all humans, although an authoritative source tells me that cats are one of the few things the French don't eat.

Cats and dogs co-exist when they have to with forbearance and weary tact.

This Yorkshire terrier is young. His favourite pastime is to threaten the elderly cat whose home he has recently invaded with fierce growls and barks designed to inspire terror but which remain coolly ignored. The cat keeps his head averted from the irritant at all times. After ten minutes of these sallies, pounces which always judiciously fall short of the cat's reach, mumbled menaces, empty challenges, hysterical defiance, the cat turns to him with a sigh, then lashes out one lightning black paw. There's a shriek and an ignominiously quick retreat, and peace returns.

This cat, while pretending to be a lump of bread pudding, is really waiting for the milkman. No one knows why cats find it necessary to keep impersonating things. And why, for example, tea-cosies, hearth-rugs, buddhas and trussed chickens? They're great parodists, too, simulating acts of reading, thought, affection and exhaustion with great skill.

OVERLEAF
Trying to train another cat to lie on the opposite side of the doorway, for heraldic effect, is hopeless. Stone lions, while more expensive initially, are much cheaper on heating, liver and legs of furniture. They don't spread cat litter or sawdust all over the place, either.

The look on a cat's face when it scratches its chin is totally devoid of charm. It's not dissimilar in its lack of allure to the glazed expression on the cat-tray. Both are good indications of a cat's intellect. When, for example, a cat looks thoughtful it means his peanut-sized brain is invariably empty.

A favourite game of this cat is to plead most pitifully to be let out of the back door, to leap immediately up to the dining-room window-sill and plead, equally pitifully, to be let in again. After half-an-hour of the "Little Match Girl" routine, the long suffering owner's favourite game is to let the little so-and-so stew.

If, having nothing better to do, you covered the floor of a room with newspaper, and then put a Daily Mail-sized piece of carpet on top of it, a cat would seek it out to lie on. Fascinating, isn't it?

A strictly-observed feline ordinance is that the lighter one's fur the more colourful the rubbish one has to doze on. This lapse in an equally strictly-observed fastidiousness is one more mystery cat lovers/sufferers ponder as they clean black footprints off pillows, windowsills, fridge doors, blouse-fronts, breakfast plates, etc.

About 7 every morning our street teems with homeward-bound cats with breakfast and radiators in their eyes. This fellow has no tail, but I don't know if he was a Manx or merely the victim of an undignified accident. He disappeared a week after this shot was taken, and no one ever saw him again.

The loss of a limb doesn't incapacitate an animal as resourceful as a cat. This one, named Juniper, can climb trees, chase rabbits feet and do everything whole cats do except wash her left side. She lives with two other cats and a dog who wash it for her. Honestly.

113

The look of rapt pleasure in this shot is due to the fact that the Tallis 40-part motet was on the radio when it was taken. The same self-indulgent languor is caused in this subject also by Count Basie, Schoenberg, The Who and Yesterday in Parliament.

When the sun comes up, cats lie down. No matter how assiduously you train them to partition their diaries sensibly, they fundamentally dislike the day. Daylight is for sleeping through, preferably undisturbed. Night beckons with an irresistible finger, a promise of liaisons, mystery, interesting sounds and smells, danger and opportunities for song. How could a cat sire a litter, torment a mouse, steal, tear up the carpet or go to the lavatory in the kitchen in the banal light of day?

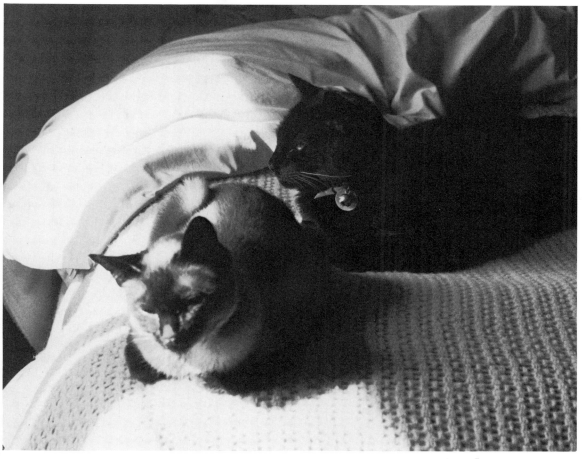

A cat with the aesthetic refinement of a lion must find his sense of propriety offended at having to languish perennially below pretending shutters. The girl is pretty, though.

Dustbins, cars, squares of earth round trees, tops of walls, these are the humble beacons that circumscribe a town cat's territory. A country cat's consists of hedgerows, haystacks, ploughs, troughs, manure, all preferable points of reference, you'd have thought. Healthier, anyway. The "good" life is a universal myth, evidently. Did you know, for instance, that, given the opportunity, town cats take readily to large gins and cigar-smoking?

OVERLEAF
Closing-time at The Crown at Holland Park is cleaning-up time. For an animal so furtive and quiet about most things, a cat's ablutions are curiously rough and audible. If you've ever let a cat sleep on your bed you'll know it always wakes about 1 a.m. for a protracted wash and brush-up. As you lie there, feeling the bed rock rhythmically, listening to the slapping, slurping sounds of a Victorian soup kitchen, you wonder why you don't get a dog instead.

119

The eccentricity of this window display caught my eye, which it was no doubt intended to do. I'm not sure why the leopard is looking up the flying skirt, though. And the cast in the reclining cat's eye presumably testifies to Siamese blood not otherwise apparent.

You may have noticed how cats excel at asking for things. No one's left in any doubt as to their wishes. If they want to come in, go out, be left alone, fed or taken notice of, their persistence is astonishing. Their creativity, too. A lot of cats, to attract attention, will do something that attracts attention. Marvellous, that. Like using the leg of a side-table as a scratching-post, especially if it's Sheraton, Dutch marquetry or Louis Quinze ormolu.

Nobody buys middle-aged cats however diligently they backlight themselves in the effort to appeal. People like the fun of kittens, not the set personalities and inflexible attitudes of mature adults. A similar predilection can be observed in men for the female of their species.

I wonder why lions became the subject of so many town knockers. Why Dolphins, too, and ladies' faces? Why not mice knockers, or winkles, rabbits or bars-of-chocolate knockers?